a novella

praise for M.F. McAuliffe's SEATTLE:

M.F. McAuliffe's *Seattle* tells the story of a bereft widow and disillusioned photographer working as a librarian at an image agency. Amid the digitally strained commerce of a photojournalism company her secretive impressions and fragmentary memories streak through the prose in poetic bursts of tension, anger and doubt. The nervous power of the writing is reminiscent of old style photography, when film would be processed in developer so that a latent image could become visible. One feels the story beneath Seattle emerging with the same chemical intensity, its meaning rising before you moment by moment.

— Mark Mordue, author, *Dastgah: Diary of A Head Trip*

McAuliffe's 25 poems on the death of ursula k. le guin

> The poems are heart-rending and at the same time full of love.
> — Luisa Valenzuela, author of *Clara, Strange Things Happen Here, The Lizard's Tail, Deathcats*

> "Each day the world got a day's worth of worse, and went on," McAuliffe writes, and this sensibility of endurance, of "climbing chalk cliffs by front teeth alone" gives us this — a particular grief, a critique and context, a poetic something-more, on the death of Ursula K. Le Guin. A monumental monument, a sending forth of some Great Ship, a pain-spattered sunset, a howling — and more.
> — Jenny Forrester, author, *Narrow River, Wide Sky,* and *A Memoir & Soft Hearted Stories: Seeking Saviors, Cowboy Stylists, and Other Fallacies of Authoritarianism*

praise for M.f. McAuliffe's CRUCIFIXES & OTHER FRI-DAY POEMS

> This book takes the reader to ancient Rome, straight from the mouth of Catullus to the person sitting right beside us. McAuliffe makes these poems relevant to everyday life in the present, yet channels ancient memories; reminding us that some things are eternal and can never leave our consciousness.
> — Amy Temple Harper, author of *Cramped Uptown*

praise for M.f. McAuliffe's SEATTLE: a novella

Back office transactions, cavernous electronic databases, suspicious dealings, duplicity, innocence, the complexities of lost love ... The controlled rage throughout *Seattle* does the memory of Mother Jones proud.

— Julie Madsen, editor, *W*O*R*K*** Magazine

A marvelous stretch of work.

— Matthew Stadler, author, *Deventer, The Dissolution of Nicholas Dee, Chloe Jarren's La Cucaracha, & Where We Live Now*

25 Poems on the Death of Ursula K. Le Guin

M. F. McAuliffe

a shoegaze book

SHOEGAZE BOOKS   ISBN 978-1-68454-471-4

$12.00

All rights reserved. No part of this book may be reproduced in any form without written permission of the copyright owners.

The images in this book have been reproduced with knowledge & prior consent of the artists concerned, & no responsibility is accepted by the producer, publisher, or printer for any infringement of copyright or otherwise, arising from the contents of this publication. Every effort has been made to ensure that credits accurately comply with information supplied. We apologize for any inaccuracies that may have occurred & will resolve inaccurate or missing information in any subsequent reprinting of the book.

10 9 8 7 6 5 4 3 2

||| Cover & Interior Design: T. Warburton y Bajo ||| Int. red star youth images: T. Warburton y Bajo ||| Cover: Pompeiian doggy, M. F. McAuliffe |||

25 POEMS ON THE DEATH OF URSULA K. LE GUIN

M. F. McAULIFFE

25: Poems on the Death of Ursula K. Le Guin
Copyright © 2019, M.F. McAULIFFE
1st. print ed., pub. Nov., 2019, Shoegaze Books,
distrib. by GobQ L.L.C., 338 NE Roth, Portland OR 97211

25 Poems on the Death of Ursula K. Le Guin

M. F. McAuliffe

a shoegaze book

– 1 –

Still near the solstice
Still near the dark
the too-early daffodils already blading
her soul became the size of the whole low grey
                        sky

And afterwards
nothing happened.

Each day
the world got a day's worth of worse,
and went on.

- 2 -

I didn't see much of your street
when I worked there, briefly, years ago:
overpass, hard light, concrete.

This morning, among the trees, by the stop
               sign
its name is an ulcer of emptiness.

– 3 –

Spring was colder than winter
and you were gone
and the rain so hard we couldn't look up,
or see you, looking sideways,
your canyons laughing
and your skies –
though it was houses you understood,
and people,

– who are mysteries –
– I'd rather watch Magellanic clouds –

Spring was colder than winter
and you were gone
though I wouldn't admit it
couldn't

But the cold is biting, and the rain rains

and I suppose something is happening
but God only knows what it is
in the grey, with you gone.

– 4 –

These hard industrial spaces
full of concrete
shrubs so hardy you can hardly stand to
                look at them
the kerb not only railing to the horizon
but discontinuous
everywhere

It's always pain-spattered sunset here
a howling

Night coming
more barren than the day
you've just passed
earth as alien as cement

– 5 –

How can the evening be mild and you not here to see it?

– 6 –

gone as her parents
gone as that whole hundred years

– 7 –

She will not be on any street
you walk on

– 8 –

Oh, Portland,
with your DIY funk
knotted streets laid out by the Corps
gnarled rooms, upstairs basements
small and hard

where nothing fits and everything is
                difficult –

– 9 –

I saw you at the Awards
you'd founded,
a shadow and
a turn of silver hair

Then, walking to the car
in the gliding air,
not satin, not silk,
damp, molecular, too well-lit,
too-warm, a melting frost of neon glare

I saw no shadow, no silver.
You were nowhere there.

– 10 –

birds glide north and south
over the mud-stopped mouth of Vesuvius

the depth of it
thick, piled-down, œsophogeal, choked
hard as a tennis court

noweepingnomemorynoloss

– 11 –

In a Pompeiian alley
a man tried to crawl
away

The mountain came to him.

– 12 –

The dog a twist of bones.

– 13 –

Sometimes
I write
on the backs
of old
paystubs
each one
half a month
of my life

I think
of you
married
then
pregnant
then
with a child

and wonder
how

in the great silence
of the rounded
rooms
of your house
you could
grasp
the threads of space
weave
time

how there could be
a life
given

not
having
to be

rented out,
½-
stolen
back

stunted at every turn:

the time it takes to make a world
windows, rain, commute,
mountains, light, sea, the creatures
in their boxes, talking

the precise
tones of the birds in the morning
so like bellbirds, so unlike

the time it takes to go and return from that
                            place,
the journey repeated
so often the door lies open
so often the wall dissolves
so often that place is real
and surprising

and the writing
controlling and refining
writes itself through you
so that the writing and the written, the

                              perceiver and the
                              perceived

are one thing
the gold in the fire
in the dark.

That is what is forbidden us
by the lack of time

That is what is forbidden all of us
the readers of other people's worlds

by drudgery,
the sink and the sinkhole.

Prices rise

Until only the secure middle class of the
                              past
could have done this
until only the 1%
can do this

until we're reduced to being grateful
for this vast historic theft;

for the occasional gifted aristocrat.

- 14 -

But this is a democracy still.

We the unconnected are encouraged to
                             address

writing
coming-of-age
family
sex
self-esteem
overcoming personal odds to live our best
                             lives
(the odds are always personal)

(talk among ourselves
mind our own business)

– 15 –

Her presence on the hill
a lamp over the city
a warmth
a warmth

– 16 –

The keys of her laptop hollowed and worn

– 17 –

Your wake approaches
as surely as your death did.

Everyone will go

so many in Hubble-image t-shirts
who you saved from their pain while they
               were reading
unpossessed, lonely and yearning

Saturday afternoons
on the soft synthetic ethnic throw
while the sun went down on the nothing
               outside,

the harsh and shadowless road unshaping
to red soil saltbush, Nullarbor, mines,
the inaudible, undeniable, underlying voice

of industrial rock, machinery,
banishment

long dark dreams
climbing chalk cliffs by front teeth alone

mornings overhung with bewilderment
roses leaching out of their petals
the flesh of the sky scraped to sunset

A mining town built
explicitly to prevent Krupp taking a lease
               in the '30s

nothing grew that Europeans would eat,
so many of them,
except South Australian whiting, gar,
               butterfish,
everything else freighted in
water two hundred miles of pump and
               pipe two foot six across

blast furnace, steelworks, shipyards
bucket of molten iron three stories high
the hills
molten steel, rolled steel, warships, ore-
                ships
became holes
and two thousand English, Welsh and
                Scottish steelworkers
dirging through "Mull of Kintyre"

all their green places
turned haematite and red.

Helpless as rock blown to gravel
(flywire screens,
cement,
weeds)

One Saturday morning
looking at my feet as I walked to the
                newsagent
thinking how to construct a book
(tiles passing under my feet)

I looked up

Student
a few feet away
the girl expelled for being pregnant
trembling smile
I hadn't known her well
I became a small tower
of embarrassment, fear, shame, guilt
I hadn't known, helped –

You could negotiate your way out if
                       you were related to the
                       Sassoons
but only one of us ever was.

What other way then but the soft ethnic
                       throw
& the extraterrestrial deep?

How can anything but a hungry god
build a cathedral?

Driving north, rounding the Gulf at its tip
Augusta a terrifying blot of despair
despite the new bridge, a shriek
vomitous to be in, guilt-making to escape
              from
spilling to and from the north, ochre, rust,
              blood, hinterland, history,
half a continent of crime hidden and
              intended and forgotten till
              that moment,
reservations for weapons research
and for the dead and their descendants

Pale yellow grass
ears and stalks
separate in the curling cold
saltwater flats leading down to salt water;

Low mountains folded like hills
dip and shadow, and the shadow leached,
and the dry
aching parch of the stretch between
the land long and nothing but rib

crumbling soil lying on nothing but rib,

Three ghost gums by the side of the road
half an hour south
marking the Goyder Line, where reliable
                farming ended.

But then through the window the intimation
the volume of shadow and fold and age
the mass of the ranges
a comfort, a sound.

One night, raining cats, dogs, cattle
the Shell station at Crystal Brook
another car, big, big,
and the bloke who ran the station,
slight, limping, overalls,
hair dripping, drenched,
hurrying to the pump while the Americans
fat imperious smug
ordered air, oil, gas,
and turned to order food from his wife
                inside

Moonglinted eyes, passing the semis
(closepacked sheep and cattle)

The lower lands only dull
shading down to saltwater most of the way
the fountain in the corner of the café in the
                     BP station at Port Wakefield,
freshwater,
the mystery of freshwater flowing into itself
in and in and through,
the only joy
from there to the Aboriginal springs
at Katherine.

Further south
horizontal gums
(bitter wind, salt wind)
the Main North Road:
abattoirs;
saleyards, tractors, combine harvesters,
                    ploughs;
Adelaide;
the labyrinthine unhappiness of home.

I never saw those northern gorges
godsword sundered sun-red rock,
cathedrals of water and silence.

I never saw you in Melbourne
didn't know you were coming
never spoke to you, argued, talked, caught
the view so clear it could comprehend
                continents
the current war, the history of logging, the
                fate of the California Indians
                reversed;
never came to inhabit your universe.

Your wake.

We have to go.
You've been kind to our House,
institution to institution.
Though we have to be seen to have been
                there
though I couldn't bear not to be there

I'm still as far from you as I ever was
on the Main North Road
a speck in the dark.

– 18 –

I'm not going to say, co-worker,
that I saw you at the wake.
My grief is ugly, angry, petty, vain,
desperate –
>It's not for your entertainment,
>you passionless stalk.

It's flesh without skin.

– 19 –

No, I'm not reading you.
I'm reading Alice Oswald
who's illuminating every death in *The Iliad*.
Yes, there are deaths in *The Iliad*, too.

I'm tired of the death here.
It's clamourous.

God, can we close the book and be done!
Close our eyes and be done

go out into the shade of trees somewhere
and listen to the quiet
fall of the light of the sun.

– 20 –

the light
coming in
at ceiling height
falling
on her skin

a shell
a shawl

lightly
drawing in

- 21 -

Looking around the library
to recommend your most sublime work
to someone who hasn't
read you before
I find books & books & books on the
     shelves
that by rights shouldn't be there,
things bought immediately after your
     death
that should still be passing
hand to hand to starving hand
and are not:
and I wonder what's wrong with people
(books aren't cheap,
even e-books aren't cheap)
much as you wondered
why you couldn't be considered for a
     Pulitzer

and it reminds me
of the strangeness of the crowd
at the wake
the absence of luminaries
at the wake

It makes me wonder
what they thought you were doing,
are,

telling tales of wizards to children
tales of détente to dragons
tales of the failure of conquest
to everyone

– 22 –

You say, "A great library is freedom."

Apart from your probably meaning
Triple-X Public, where I've worked for
                twenty years,
and know for a fact to be run by the vicious
undergirded by the clueless, or vice versa,
                depending on the regime

I say freedom is far more

Freedom is being free to use a great library
without bargaining your right to eat or
                sleep
to do it

the place being inhabited more by the
                homeless than by scholars

than by the dignified poor, carefully clothed
(mentally but not physically starved)
(this is not the '30s; this is not the movies)

the place a temporary shelter from the great
              predations of the State-backed
              anarchy of cash:

lying cylindrical in sleeping bags
across the footpaths in winter
freezing

dead in a bus shelter
a baby
3 plastic sheets to the wind

human turds extruded & excluded.

I know you know this

I'm weary with seeing the machine & what it
              does

Great libraries are great –

                (the paperback rack at Safeway
                among the mid-County car-yards)

Freedom is people racking off
leaving you
alone to get on with it
enough light and peace to get on with it

enough distance from your situation to be able
                to see it & act upon it
    (sometimes the only freedom you've got is
                your own desperation)

Your forgiveness stories
The Yeowe and Werel slave stories
I didn't find visionary
though they became sublime
I found them odd,
living there already

Below you is where the slaves live

Perhaps you are right
& having no real choice

is not the same as being locked up
held in bondage, tortured, set to prostitution

The slaves live below us

But that's where it starts
with the predilection,
with the desire
for close-quarter control over someone else's
                yes or no.

"A job that's neither
exhausting nor morally disgusting,"
a friend once said to me,
smiling because I'd finally found work I could
                do.
But it is exhausting now
& a lot less not morally disgusting than it used
                to be

Context is everything
feeling has always been the difference between
   marriage, prostitution, and bond-servitude

Let me tell you a story.

Once upon a time a great library
had clever, intelligent, highly-skilled
                librarians
and said:
You will be replaced by your assistants.
Said to the assistants:
Don't tell us what won't work.
Chop-chop
lickety-split robo-grind
is the best you can hope for

if you don't want
(human turd)

if you don't want
(bus shelter)

If a great library is freedom
Whose freedom is it?

– 23 –

There is no community.
I quarrel with the dead.

– 24 –

I go on
go on
go on

the street-maples grow, canopy-wise
the hawks rise through their clear chasms,
               screaming

– 25 –

It's been a sickly autumn –
December,
and dead leaves
still hanging on the trees,
the sky straight blue at dawn,
dark, torn-winged seeds rattling along the
        broom-stroke,
multi-seed pods mummifying on branches
        beyond identification.
The wind would be cruel if there were any.
The air is motionless and still.

*– for
Ursula*

M. F. McAuliffe was born & educated in Adelaide and Melbourne, has an Honours degree in English & graduate work in photography, film, & anthropology. In 2002 she co-founded the multi-lingual, award-winning, Portland-based magazine, *Gobshite Quarterly* with RV Branham, & continues there as co-editor.

She made her US debut in Damon Knight's *Clarion Awards*, & has since co-authored *Fighting Monsters* (with Judith Steele, Melbourne, 1998), the artist's book *Golems Waiting Redux* (with Daniel Duford, Portland, 2011), & supplied the libretto for La Mama Courthouse's production *Orpheus: an Australian Tragedy* (Carlton, 2000); the text of *Crucifix i.*, along with a photograph, appear in the Yoko Ono-curated installation, "Arising", 7 Oct., 2016 through 5 Feb., 2017, at Reykjavik Art Museum. She is currently editing & publishing some titles for Reprobate/GobQ Books. Her most recent book is *I'm Afraid of Americans*, from shoegaze.

a **shoegaze** book

also available, from yr bookstore,
or from gobshitequarterly.com:

I'M AFRAID OF AMERICANS: STORIES, M F MCAULIFFE, SHOEGAZE BOOKS, ISBN 978-1-9442444I-5, $16.00

SEATTLE: a novella, M. F. McAULIFFE, SHOEGAZE BOOKS, ISBN 978-1-9442444I-5, $14.00

Other titles will appear soonerish rather than laterish...

we'll meet again...
don't know how, don't know when...

www.ingramcontent.com/pod-product-compliance
Lightning Source LLC
LaVergne TN
LVHW011858060526
838200LV00054B/4400